Collective Biographies

AMERICAN WOMEN INVENTORS

Carole Ann Camp

Enslow Publishers, Inc.

40 Industrial Road	PO Box 38
Box 398	Aldershot
Berkeley Heights, NJ 07922	Hants GU12 6BP
USA	UK

http://www.enslow.com

To my brother, Floyd

Library of Congress Cataloging-in-Publication Data

Camp, Carole Ann.
    American Women Inventors / by Carole Ann Camp.
        p. cm. — (Collective Biographies)
    Includes bibliographical references and index.
    Summary: Ten biographies of American women inventors, including Madam
C. J. Walker, Lillian Gilbreth, Beulah Henry, Elizabeth Lee Hazen , Rachel Fuller
Brown, Katherine Blodgett, Gertrude B. Elion, Stephanie Louise Kwolek, Edith
Flanigen, and Ellen Ochoa.
    ISBN 0-7660-1913-6
    1. Women inventors—United States—Biography—Juvenile literature. [1.
Inventors. 2. Women—Biography.} 1. Title. II. Series.
    T39.C36 2002
    609.2'273—dc21

                                                    2001006703

Printed in the United States of America

10 9 8 7 6 5 4 3 2

To Our Readers:
We have done our best to make sure all Internet addresses in this book were active and
appropriate when we went to press. However, the author and the publisher have no
control over and assume no liability for the material available on those Internet sites
or on other Web sites they may link to. Any comments or suggestions can be sent by
e-mail to comments@enslow.com or to the address on the back cover.

Every effort has been made to locate all copyright holders of material used in this
book. If any errors or omissions have occurred, corrections will be made in future
editions of this book.

Illustration Credits: U. S. Patent Office: pp. 11, 14; ArtToday.com: p. 85;
Clipart.com: p. 32; Brigham's and Women's Hospital: p.69; Courtesy of the
Dupont Company: pp. 72, 76; Library of Congress: pp. 18, 26, 54; NASA:
pp. 88, 93; National Archives: p. 60; Scientific American: pp. 36, 40;
Wadsworth Center, New York State Department of Health: p. 44;
Webnoises.com: p. 80

Cover Illustration: Ellen Ochoa: NASA; Madam C. J. Walker, Katherine
Blodgett: Library of Congress; Stephanie Kwolek: Courtesy of the Dupont
Company

Contents

Introduction

Who was the first inventor? Who was the first woman inventor? Who was the first American woman inventor? It is impossible to answer these questions. Men and women have been inventing since the dawn of human civilization. Some inventions have lasted throughout history, like the invention of the wheel, while other inventions served their purpose for a short time and became artifacts in a museum, like the butter churn. Some inventors became very famous, such as Thomas Edison, and some remained in obscurity, as did Hannah Slater.

Women have always invented things, especially things historically related to women's lives, like articles of clothing and household gadgets. However, women have not received the credit for their inventions. One of the problems with trying to set the record straight is that the U.S. patent office did not come into existence in the United States until 1790.

A patent is a government document that gives the inventor exclusive rights to his or her new and useful invention. A patent protects the inventor from other people making, using, selling, or importing the invention for a period of time. The patent protection lasts for twenty years from the date the inventor applied for the patent.

When the patent office was established, there were no written rules saying that women could not file for a patent. In the early years, unfortunately, many factors worked against women applying for patents. In some cases, women believed that "it just was not done," or it was not "lady-like."[1] In other situations, it was considered natural for the man who was the head of the household to file for the patent, even if a woman had been the inventor.

Another problem that faced both men and women inventors was the expense of filing for a patent. They often had to hire lawyers to do research on patents that already existed. The inventor had to make sure that the new invention was not a duplication of an invention that already had a patent. This has always been a costly and timely business. In the early days of the United States, women did not own property or have bank accounts in their own names. It was often very difficult for women to acquire the money necessary to hire a lawyer and to apply for a patent.

Beginning in the middle of the 1800s, women's names start to appear in the patent records in their own right. Historians have identified over fifteen hundred patents issued to women between 1865 and 1900.[2] While many women's names appear in the records, the stories about their lives remain a mystery. It was the world's fairs, especially the 1876 Centennial Exposition in Philadelphia and the 1893 Columbian Exposition in Chicago, that showcased exhibitions of inventions by women.[3]

Many African-American women have also been inventors, but their stories are even more difficult to uncover. Slaves did not have the means to file for patents. They had no financial support and no easy way to file. In addition, because race was not one of the questions listed on the patent application, it is difficult to know if the applicants were African Americans or not.

People can apply for a patent, not only for a tangible gadget like a can opener, but also for an idea or a new way of doing something. Sometimes people create things only when they see a need. Sometimes people just notice something unusual in what they are doing. Other people develop or invent processes or equipment in the course of their everyday work. With the introduction of computer technology into modern society, the opportunities for creation and invention have skyrocketed. Just as human beings have been inventors since the beginning of time, human beings will continue to be inventors until the end of time. The stories of the women in this book are only a minute sample of the stories of the thousands of women who have contributed to the advancement of human society through their creativity and their inventions.

The First American
Women Inventors

The stories of many of the first American women inventors have been lost. Some of the descriptions of their inventions survive in the records of the U.S. Patent and Trademark Office (USPTO), but the life stories of these inventors have not survived.

Possibly, the first American women inventor to file for a patent in the United States was Hannah Slater. Almost nothing is known of her life, except that she was the wife of the famous Samuel Slater, sometimes referred to as the father of the American Industrial Revolution. He started the spinning industry in Rhode Island. Hannah Slater filed for a patent under the name of Mrs. Samuel Slater in 1797 for a new way to spin thread.[1]

Many other women inventors, both with and without patents, created products and processes that made tedious tasks easier. Only a few of these women are included in this chapter, but many more could have been.

Mary Kies (18th-19th Century)

Many researchers record Mary Kies of Killingly, Connecticut, as the first American female patent holder.[2] On May 15, 1809, she received a patent for a method of weaving straw with silk or thread to create bonnets. Some believe that her invention was not for an object, like the bonnet, but rather for a process of weaving. Others believe that her invention was for some kind of machine that wove straw and silk together in a unique and special way. In any case, her invention was timely. The young United States was trying to become self-sufficient by not relying totally on foreign goods. Mary Kies contributed to the early industrialization of New England and the American Industrial Revolution. The hats and bonnets created by her process competed favorably with hats and bonnets imported from Europe. She established a very successful hat- and bonnet-producing industry. Upon hearing of Kies's industry, Dolley Madison, the wife of President Madison, sent Kies a letter of congratulations.[3]

Unfortunately, a fire in the patent office in 1836 destroyed the exact details of Mary Kies's invention.

Margaret Knight (1838–1914)

Margaret Knight was born in York, Maine, in 1838. Her family moved to Manchester, New Hampshire, where she attended elementary school. She always enjoyed playing with woodworking toys and other machinelike gadgets.

When she was ten years old, she worked in a cotton mill with her brothers. While working there, she witnessed a serious accident. She wanted to help prevent similar accidents. When she was twelve, she created a machine to make the weaving of cotton safer. Her invention caused the machines to stop quickly when they malfunctioned. The mill owners put her invention to work right away and it saved many lives.[4]

When she moved to Springfield, Massachusetts, Knight worked for the Columbia Paper Bag Company. Paper bags made at this time looked like envelopes and were not very useful for carrying bulky items. While working there in 1867, she invented a machine that would cut, fold, and paste a bag with square bottoms. She worked for two years on her invention. She experimented on many wooden models before trying out a metal version of her machine.

In the meantime, another inventor, Charles Annan, copied her design and filed for the patent of the flat-bottomed paper bag-folding machine. Knight took Annan to court at considerable expense to herself. Annan told the court that a woman could not possibly understand how to make a machine. The court, however, recognized that Knight was the real inventor and voted in her favor. She received her patent in 1871.[5]

Knight paid the Ames Manufacturing Company in Chicopee, Massachusetts, to manufacture her paper bag-folding machines. With her machine, she was able to establish the Eastern Paper Bag Company to produce and sell the first flat-bottomed paper bags.

Knight patented at least twenty-six other inventions, many used in industry. She also invented machines and gadgets that she never patented. Among her inventions are machines for shoe production, household items, parts of the internal combustion engine, and a window frame and sash.

The details of the rest of Knight's life are lost. Nobody knows why, but in 1914, Margaret Knight died in poverty.

Sara E. Goode (Sarah Good) (19th Century)

Sara Goode was probably the first African-American woman to receive a patent. Because the application for a patent did not indicate inventors' race, it is possible that other African-American women received patents before she did. Sara Goode owned a furniture store in Chicago in the 1880s. She invented a bed that would conserve space. During the day, her invention looked like and functioned as an ordinary desk.

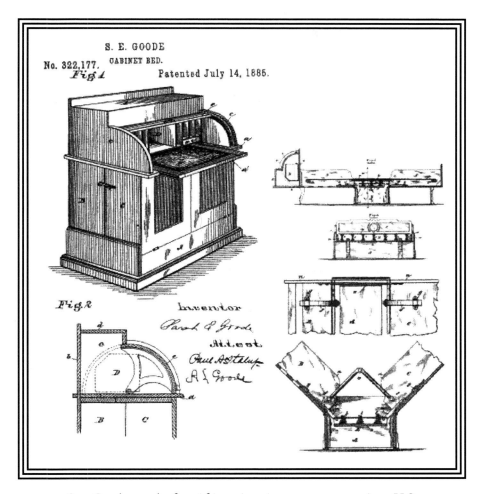

Sara Goode was the first African-American woman to receive a U.S. patent. This is a drawing of her invention, the cabinet bed. The drawing was part of her patent application.

At night, the desk turned into a foldout bed. It was the prototype for many other foldaway beds in use today. She received Patent #322,177 for the cabinet bed on July 14, 1885.

Miriam Benjamin (1861–?)

Miriam Benjamin was born in 1861, the daughter of Eliza Clausen, a free African American and Mr. Benjamin, (his first name is unknown), a white plantation owner. At the end of the Civil War and on the death of Benjamin, Eliza Clausen took Miriam and her three other children to Boston, Massachusetts, with the money she had inherited from Benjamin. Miriam attended school and eventually earned her teaching degree. Leaving Boston, she taught school in Charlestown, South Carolina, for three years. After moving back to Boston, and then New York City, Miriam Benjamin finally settled in Washington, D.C., to continue her teaching career. It was during this time that she invented the Gong and Signal Chair. This chair would allow a person to signal that they needed assistance from someone by pressing a button. The chair was soon installed in the House of Representatives and Senate for the use of congressmen. It proved to be the predecessor to the signaling system still being used in passenger airplanes. She received Patent #386,289 on July 17, 1888. About her patent she said:

My invention relates to certain new and useful improvements in gong and signal chairs to be used in dining rooms, in hotels, restaurants, steamboats, railroad trains, theaters, the hall of congress of the United States, the halls of the legislatures of the various states for the use of all deliberative bodies, and for the use of invalids in hospitals.[6]

No other details of Miriam Benjamin's life have been discovered.

Sarah Boone (1839–1904)

Sarah Marshall was born on April 2, 1839, to James Marshall and Sarah Morgan in New Bern, North Carolina, as a free African American. She married James Boone when she was thirteen. In 1868, Sarah and James Boone moved to New Haven, Connecticut, with their eight children. Sarah Boone's husband died in 1876. In order to support herself and her youngest daughter, she became a dressmaker. In the process of making dresses, she decided that she needed a special kind of ironing board to press the collars and cuffs of the dresses more easily. She invented a type of ironing board to make the ironing process easier and more efficient. She received the patent for her ironing board in 1892. Sarah Boone died on October 29, 1904 of kidney disease in New Haven, Connecticut.[7]

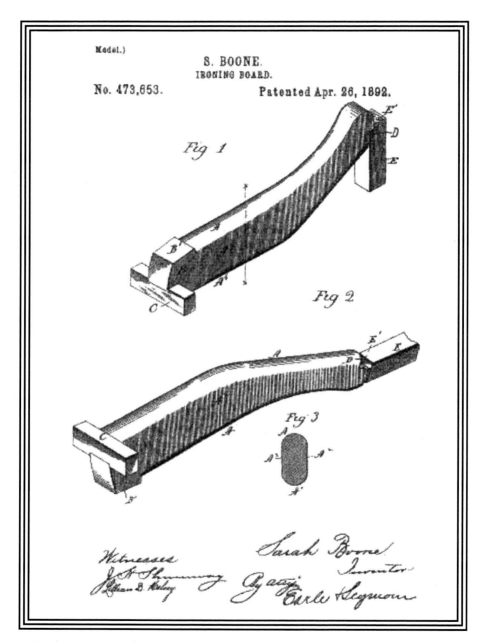

Sarah Boone earned a patent for her invention of a special type of ironing board.

Mary Anderson (1866–1953)

Mary Anderson was born in Alabama in 1866. Her aunt had died and had left Mary some money. With the money, she took a trip to New York City. During her visit, it snowed. It was the first time she had ever seen snow. While she was riding on the trolley during the snowstorm, she watched as the trolley driver put his arm out of the window continuously to try to scrape the snow off the windshield.

To prevent ice from forming on the windshields, trolley motormen had to keep rubbing the glass with damp tobacco or a cut onion. This created a film on the glass which was supposed to keep ice crystals from forming. It was a very cold process and not very effective.

Anderson had an idea. She found a piece of paper in her handbag and drew a picture of a mechanical arm operated from the inside of the trolley. Her invention had a long, scraping arm attached to the outside of the window. This arm was connected to a handle on the inside of the trolley, which the trolley driver could easily reach and turn. By turning the handle on the inside, the trolley driver could make the windshield wiper move back and forth on the outside. The trolley driver could stay warm and the process was easier and much more effective.[8]

Fighting against her friends' joking and kidding, Anderson received a patent for the windshield wiper in 1903. She tried to sell her invention to a manufacturing company, but at first no one would buy it. One company told her that her invention had very little commercial value. The small inheritance from her aunt was not big enough to bring her windshield wiper into production without the help of a large manufacturing company. She felt rejected and discouraged and gave up trying to get her invention produced. With the production of assembly-line Model T Fords, that changed. Soon all new automobiles were equipped with windshield wipers.

Madam C. J. Walker
(1867–1919)
Hair Products Manufacturer

From a penniless orphan to a multimillionaire, Madam C. J. Walker is a classic example of the rags to riches story. Her life story is important because she accomplished her success at a time in history when it was not easy to be a woman or an African American.

Born Sarah Breedlove on December 23, 1867 to former slaves, Owen and Minerva Breedlove of Louisiana, Sarah was the first child in the family to be born free. After the end of the Civil War, the Breedloves remained on the plantation where they had been slaves. The family worked as sharecroppers. At age six, Sarah worked in the fields along with the rest of her family.

When Sarah was seven years old, her mother died. Less than two years later, her father also died.

Madam C. J. Walker

She went to live with her sister and brother-in-law, but their home was not a happy place for Sarah. After eight years, at the age of sixteen, she married Moses McWilliams and soon gave birth to her daughter, Lelia (she changed her name to A'Lelia years later). Sarah's husband died when she was twenty, leaving her penniless and with a young child. When she heard that life was better for African Americans up north, she and her daughter moved to St. Louis, Missouri.

Like many other African-American women at the time, she became a laundress. Sarah promised herself that her daughter would have a better life and would go to college. Sarah had little formal education herself when she was growing up, but she wanted to educate herself. After working at least fourteen hours a day doing other people's washing, she attended night classes at the local high school. Every week she saved part of her meager wages for A'Lelia's education. She saved enough for her daughter to go to Knoxville College.

St. Louis was a bustling, thriving community in the early 1900s. In 1904, the World's Fair came to town. With the fair came many African-American intellectuals who gave talks. For the first time, Sarah McWilliams was exposed to something other than washing clothes. Mrs. Booker T. Washington, wife of the African-American educator, impressed her the most. Even though McWilliams was already thirty-seven years old at the time, she knew that she could be more than just a laundress. The way Mrs. Washington looked—dressed up with makeup and beautifully styled hair—impressed McWilliams. She had never before seen an African-American woman dressed so attractively. At that moment, McWilliams decided to change how she looked.[1]

Sarah McWilliams, like so many other African-American women, suffered from a scalp condition that caused baldness. This condition occurred because African-American women had overused hair-straightening remedies, had poor diets, and generally suffered from poor health. Sarah McWilliams wanted to stop her hair from falling out and to heal her scalp condition, but nothing she tried worked. She said, "During my many years of research endeavoring to find something to improve my own hair, in preparations manufactured by others, I was always unsuccessful."[2]

Searching for just the right ingredients for her shampoos, she claimed that the right formula came to her in a dream. "For one night I had a dream, and in that dream a big black man appeared to me and told me what to mix for my hair. Some of the remedy was from Africa, but I sent for it, mixed it, put it on my scalp and in a few weeks my hair was coming in faster than it had ever fallen out."[3]

McWilliams started making her hair products to sell to the other African-American women in her community. Soon she had a thriving business. In 1905, McWilliams wanted to manufacture her

The
Walker
company also made
many creams,
powders, and
soaps.

As an ad for Madam C. J. Walker's products from 1920 read: "If you want beauty of complexion and loveliness of hair, try Mme. C. J. Walker's world of renowned toilet preparations."

products on a larger scale. She also decided to move her hair products company to Denver, Colorado, where her newly widowed sister-in-law and nieces lived. A'Lelia was away at college, and McWilliams believed that she would have a fresh start with her new company in Denver. Just as St. Louis had been at the edge of the frontier twenty years earlier, Denver became the bustling frontier town of the new century—the perfect place to start a new career.

With less than two dollars to her name, she moved to Denver. Working as a cook by day, and experimenting at home every night with different kinds of shampoos and conditioners, she perfected three products: Wonderful Hair Grower, Glossine, and Vegetable Shampoo.[4] Her treatment for the scalp disease consisted of frequent shampoos, a special ointment of petroleum jelly and sulfur as a conditioner, and frequent brushings.[5] She sold her products door-to-door, but only to women in the African-American communities.

Shortly after she had moved to Denver, a friend from St. Louis, Charles J. Walker, also moved to Denver. They soon married and established the Madam C. J. Walker Manufacturing Company. She selected the name because she thought it sounded impressive. From that moment on, she became Madam Walker. Within a year, she put her daughter, A'Lelia, who had just graduated from college, in charge of the Denver factory producing the hair products.

One of the problems Madam Walker faced was how to sell her products. White storeowners did not want to stock products for African Americans. She needed a way to sell her products without selling through the white-owned stores, so she invented her own way of selling. She hired and trained hundreds of African-American women to sell her products door-to-door in the African-American communities around the country.

She also traveled throughout the United States, Central America, and the West Indies advertising her products and teaching her methods of selling. Walker had very little formal education, but people enjoyed her as a dynamic, if not flamboyant, speaker. She said, "There is no flower-strewn path to success and if there is, I have not found it for if I have accomplished anything in life it is because I have been willing to work hard."[6]

Walker and her husband began to have disagreements about how to run the business. Charles wanted the business to remain small, but Sarah wanted a national organization. They could not reconcile their differences and divorced in 1912, when she was forty-five years old. In spite of the divorce, she maintained the name Madam C. J. Walker and her business prospered.

Walker continued to have dreams of expansion. She wanted to hire poor African-American women who had very little future in other unskilled jobs and train them as agents to sell her products. Eventually she managed to see her dream come true. Business was very good. She owned one of the most successful African-American businesses in the country.

By 1917, the Madam C. J. Walker Manufacturing Company grew into a multimillion dollar business employing over one thousand production workers and twenty thousand agents. They had offices in Denver and Pittsburgh with the corporate offices in Indianapolis, Indiana. She and her daughter also opened a stylish salon in Harlem at the height of the Harlem Renaissance, a time during the 1920s when African-American culture, art, music, and poetry flourished.

One of Walker's greatest contributions was to the field of marketing. Walker not only invented and manufactured hair and beauty products, but she also taught women how to sell the products. *The Walker Method* of selling was well known around the country. She established schools where women learned how to treat and take care of hair. They also took classes on how to sell the products.

Walker created the Madam C. J. Walker Hair Culturist Union of America in 1916. At the conventions, women gathered and shared their experiences and learned new skills and techniques. *The Walker Method* was the forerunner of strategies used by the Avon and Mary Kay companies today.

With the success of her business, Walker built a mansion near the Hudson River in New York. She wanted whites and African Americans to know that it was possible for African Americans to accomplish their dreams as well as succeed in business. Her house and lifestyle became an inspiration for others.

Walker was very generous with the money she made from her company. She donated great sums to groups providing educational opportunities for African Americans. Outraged by the treatment of African Americans in the south by the Ku Klux Klan, she visited the White House to protest the all-too-frequent lynchings.

Madam C. J. Walker, the first African-American woman millionaire, died of kidney failure on May 25, 1919. She was only fifty-two. About her own life she said, "I am a woman who came from the cotton fields of the South. From there, I was promoted to the washtub. From there I was promoted to the cook kitchen. And from there I promoted myself into the business of manufacturing hair goods and preparations. . . . I have built my own factory on my own ground."[7] W. E. B. Du Bois, writer and educator, wrote in his obituary of her: "It is given to few persons to transform a people in a generation. Yet this was done by the late Madam C. J. Walker."[8]

Dr. Lillian Gilbreth (left) confers with Arthur Woods, director of President Herbert Hoover's Emergency Committee for Employment in 1930. Dr. Gilbreth was in charge of women's activities in the campaign to relieve unemployment.

Lillian Gilbreth
(1878–1972)
Industrial Management Engineer

Today a growing field of industrial engineering is ergonomics. This is the study of the interaction of the worker to the work. It includes the relationship of the body to the workstation, the equipment, and the tools. Lillian Moller Gilbreth and her husband, Frank, pioneers in time and motion studies, were the grandparents of the ergonomic movement.

Throughout her life, Lillian Gilbreth devoted her creative talents to making work more enjoyable for workers and more productive for management by decreasing worker fatigue and stress.

Lillian Moller was born on May 24, 1878, in Oakland, California, to Ann and William Moller. Both Ann and William were children of German immigrants. Lillian was the oldest child in a large family of nine children. Lillian's father owned several shoe stores in the San Francisco area. Her mother ran the family household.

Before Lillian, Ann Moller had given birth to a son who only lived a few days. Ann never really regained her health after the tragic loss of her first baby. Consequently, as the oldest child in the family, the responsibility for helping with the rest of the children and for doing most of the household management fell to Lillian.

Because her mother was sickly, Lillian was always afraid that her mother might die. This caused her to be reluctant to let her mother out of her sight. Lillian's fear made her intensely shy. She was so shy, she was afraid to go to school. Lillian stayed home and had lessons with her mother and other tutors. One of her favorite activities was reading. She also developed a love of music, even though she did not like her piano teacher, who continuously hit her on the knuckles with a pencil.[1]

After high school, Lillian attended the University of California at Berkeley. She thought she wanted to study to become a teacher, so she majored in English literature. To help herself overcome her shyness, she joined the drama society and acted in several plays.

In 1900, in spite of her intense shyness, she accepted the invitation to be the first woman to deliver the commencement speech at Berkeley. In her speech, entitled "Life—A Means or an End," she suggested that humans should live life fully each day and not worry about spending all of one's life planning for the future.[2]

Lillian wanted to continue her study of English literature with Brander Matthews, a professor at Columbia University in New York City. However, he would not allow women in his classes. Disappointed, she changed her major to study for a master's degree in psychology. Unfortunately, Lillian became ill with pleurisy, a lung disease, and had to return home to California after only one year. She later completed her master's degree in English literature at Berkeley in 1902.

Before starting her doctoral studies, she celebrated finishing her work on her master's degree by joining a group of women friends on a tour of Europe. On the way, they stopped in Boston, Massachusetts. While there, she met Frank Gilbreth, who owned a very successful construction company. They fell in love. After she returned from Europe, they became engaged. They married on October 19, 1904.

Frank Gilbreth continued his construction business, traveling around the country to oversee different building projects. Sometimes he traveled more than thirty thousand miles a year. He also toured extensively in Europe, delivering lectures and attending conferences. Lillian accompanied him on many occasions.

The Gilbreths moved to Providence, Rhode Island. In order to help her husband in his business, Lillian Gilbreth continued her work for a doctoral degree at Brown University in Providence. She changed her major back to psychology, which both Frank and Lillian thought would be more useful for their business.

In addition to studying for her classes, she continued to work with her husband, refining motion study techniques and raising a family. By 1915, when she graduated from Brown, she had given birth to five girls and two boys, with another boy on the way. Mary, her second daughter, had died from diphtheria in 1911 at the age of five.

The Gilbreths worked together and developed a new system of management. They became pioneering leaders in time and motion management studies. Instead of treating workers like machines, the Gilbreths encouraged managers to communicate with their workers. They believed that the workers would be more productive if they were happy and comfortable in their work.

The study of motion techniques for eliminating physical and emotional stress in the workplace provided workers with what Lillian Gilbreth coined later as "happiness minutes." Two of the goals of motion studies were to eliminate fatigue and increase the number of happiness minutes.

The year 1919 brought more changes to the family. They moved to Montclair, New Jersey. Their tenth child was born that same year.

The Gilbreths not only tried to improve the working conditions in industry and business, they also made improvements in the home environment. With such a large family, the Gilbreths had the perfect opportunity to do research on how to run a household most effectively. They watched how their family worked. For example, they counted how many motions it took for the children to do dishes. Then they developed ways to decrease the amount of effort required to wash dishes. They designed ways to reduce the number of motions the children used to brush their hair and teeth. This research in motion studies led them to develop a variety of other ways to help homemakers and families function more smoothly.

In 1924, two years after their twelfth child was born, Frank Gilbreth died. Lillian Gilbreth now had to support her large family, including paying college tuition for the older children. She continued working in the field of management studies after the death of her husband. She planned and led workshops in industrial management, attracting students from around the world.

At first, some of the leaders in the industrial community were reluctant to hire her, but she persevered. She soon developed her own reputation as an expert in industrial management. Following in her husband's footsteps, she continued to travel extensively around the world giving lectures and attending meetings.

During the Depression years that followed World War II, many businesses were devastated, but Gilbreth's business flourished. Factory owners, who

One of Dr. Gilbreth's inventions that is probably used every day around the world is the step-on lid-opening trash can. Her invention made it easier to dispose of trash.

were struggling to find ways to save money, hired Lillian Gilbreth. She helped them design more efficient and healthier work environments. Later, in order to demonstrate her own theory that management should learn from the workers, Gilbreth worked in Macy's department store as a clerk. She believed that this was the best way to learn how the work actually flowed and how to make improvements. Macy's was so impressed with her suggestions that they hired her to train all of the workers.

Gilbreth helped homemakers by redesigning kitchens and household appliances that saved both time and money. She patented many household devices to make the homemaker's work easier.

One invention is the step-on lid-opening trash can. She also invented an electric food mixer.[3] Her published articles on home-improvements span several decades with *The Home-Maker and Her Job* in 1927 to *Management in the Home* in 1954. She also focused on improving and redesigning kitchens for people with physically challenging conditions.

Leading the way for future women engineers, in 1926 she became the first woman member of the American Society of Mechanical Engineers. Throughout her life, she received many awards and honors. In 1930, President Herbert Hoover asked her to be in charge of the women's activities for the president's Emergency Committee for Employment. She designed the "Share the Work" program that was very successful across the country.[4] Several other presidents also enlisted her help. Over the years, she served on many national committees including civil defense, war production, aging, and rehabilitation of the physically challenged.

She taught courses at a variety of colleges and universities. In 1935, she became professor of Management at Purdue University. Later, during World War II, she served as a management consultant in many factories around the country that were making war materials.

Lillian Gilbreth received her first honorary degree in 1928 from the University of Michigan. Over twenty honorary degrees followed. In 1959, the Industrial Management Society named her "Mother of the Year." In 1984 the United States Post Office issued a stamp honoring her. A popular movie, called *Cheaper by the Dozen*, based on a book by the same title, chronicles some of the stories of the Gilbreth family.

After a very productive and happy life, Lillian Gilbreth died in 1972. She lived up to her commencement speech at Berkeley by living her life fully each day and not worrying about the future. Lillian Gilbreth showed the world how to increase the "happiness minutes" in one's life.

Beulah Henry
(1887–1973)
Multitalented Inventor

Beulah Henry invented so many different things that some called her "the Lady Edison."[1] Although her name appears on at least forty-nine patents, there is little information about her childhood and even these few stories do not agree. Some sources claim that she was born in Memphis, Tennessee,[2] while others claim Raleigh, North Carolina, sometime around 1887.[3]

The Social Security records have a Beulah Henry born on September 28, 1887, in Raleigh, North Carolina, to Walter Richmond Henry and Beulah Williamson Holden. She may also have been a descendant of Patrick Henry, a famous patriot of the American colonial period and the Revolutionary War. Beulah grew up in an artistic family. Her father

Beulah Henry poses with one of her many inventions, the Miss Illusion doll.

enjoyed art and her mother was an artist. Her brother wrote songs, and Beulah sketched inventions.

In 1909, Beulah Henry went to Presbyterian and Elizabeth Colleges in Raleigh, North Carolina. Although there is no record, she may have received a degree in liberal arts.[4] She never married and from the 1920s on lived in various hotels in New York City.

Henry held forty-nine patents, however, historians credit her with over one hundred inventions. She did not concentrate in one field but designed inventions for use in business as well as the home. She even invented several toys. Henry was twenty-five when she received her first patent in 1912. This patent was for an ice-cream freezer, which she may have started designing when she was fifteen.[5]

She not only invented, but she also manufactured many of her inventions. When she was thirty-seven, she said, "I have my inventions patented in four different countries and I am the president of two newly incorporated companies."[6] These companies manufactured her inventions.

Henry always claimed that she had no mechanical ability. She told a reporter, "I know nothing about mechanical terms and am afraid I do make it rather difficult for the draughtsmen to whom I explain my ideas . . ."[7] To overcome her feeling of a lack of mechanical ability, she surrounded herself with skilled mechanics, draftsmen, and production assistants.

For someone who claimed not to have any mechanical ability, she still was able to take her inventions from the first concept to the final product with skill. She said, "I am an inspirational inventor. I get a complete picture in my mind of what the invention will be like when it is finished and then set to work to get my model-maker to create a model to fit my mind's picture. Inventing is really easy; it's the development work that is heart-breaking."[8] Henry said that ideas for inventions just popped into her mind. She told an interviewer when asked why she invented things, "I invent because I cannot help it."[9]

Covering a span of over fifty years, Henry continued to design new products and to patent some of her inventions. In 1929, she designed a sponge for children called the Dolly Dip. The sponge, shaped like a doll, had a pocket. The parent put soap into the doll's pocket. This made it easier and more fun for children to wash when they took baths.

In 1935, Henry designed the Miss Illusion doll. The doll had eyes that could change color. The eyes also closed when the child held the doll horizontally. The doll looked as if she had actually fallen asleep. In addition, the doll came with different wigs; one brown and one blond. Henry created many different kinds of toys and games for children. One of her games was a Kiddie Klock. This clock taught children how to tell time. She also designed a board game called Cross Country that helped children learn about geography. These games made learning fun.

The invention that Henry liked the best was her Milka-Moo. Another toy for children, Milka-Moo was a little cow that the child could "milk." The toy had a rubber udder, which could be filled with milk. The toy cow also mooed.[10]

In addition to toys, Henry invented many items for the home. Among a variety of sewing machine related accessories, she invented the first bobbinless sewing machine (1940), a method for forming seams, and one for forming lockstitches. Henry also invented several variations on the can opener (1956) as she continued to improve on earlier models.

In the field of business, Henry received at least eleven patents spanning over thirty years. Long before copy machines came into existence, Henry created and patented a form of photocopying (1932). Her Protograph—an attachment to the typewriter— could make four copies of a document without using carbon paper. This later became important during World War II. Because of the war, carbon used in carbon paper was difficult to get. People were able to use Henry's Protograph to make several copies at once without using up the limited and precious supply of carbon.

Another of her unique inventions for the world of business was a way to attach envelopes to one another in a continuous stream. This made it easier for machines to address the envelopes and for people to do mass mailings. She received this patent in 1952.

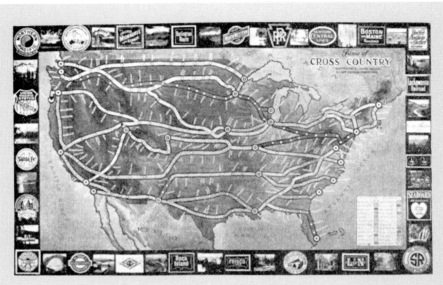

The Cross Country Board Game

The Latho rubber sponge that holds soap, a predecessor of Dolly Dips.

The "snappon" umbrella

Henry experienced one of her biggest successes with a unique style of umbrella. Instead of having just one color of material for an umbrella, Henry found a way to change the colors and the designs on the fabrics of the umbrella with interchangeable snap-on covers. In this way, people could easily match their umbrellas to the colors of their clothes. At first, manufacturers told her that it was impossible to put the snaps on the material. However, she did not give up her idea. Then the solution popped into her head at a party. She said:

> I was putting my gloves on when that snapper in all its details visualized itself against a green drapery. That ended the theater party. Mother wanted to know if I was ill, but I told her it was only the snapper and I asked her to excuse me because I just had to sketch it out on paper before I should forget. Now I have the snappers patented, also the little steel pincers that fasten the seams to the frame.[11]

Henry's umbrellas were a success and sold in some of the finest stores in the country. The stylish Lord and Taylor's department store in New York City even chose to display the umbrellas in their front window.

In addition to the time spent developing and manufacturing her many inventions, Beulah Henry held memberships in a number of organizations, including the Museum of Natural History, the

Audubon Society, and the League for Animals, which show her wide range of interests.

Beulah Henry died in New York in February 1973 at the age of eighty-five. She was a successful inventor as well as a productive member of the business community.

Elizabeth Lee Hazen
(1885–1975)
Microbiologist

Rachel Fuller Brown
(1898–1980)
Chemist

A team of two women researchers, one a microbiologist and one a chemist, made important contributions to the field of medicine at a time when there were few women scientists. Amazingly, they worked in cities far apart from each other, requiring a real team effort. Among their many inventions in the field of drugs and medicines, Elizabeth Hazen and Rachel Brown discovered nystatin, an anti-fungal medication.

Elizabeth Lee Hazen, left, and Rachel Fuller Brown.

Elizabeth Lee Hazen

On August 24, 1885, Elizabeth Lee Hazen was born in Rich, a small rural town in Mississippi, where her parents worked as cotton farmers. Before she was four years old, both of her parents died. Lee, as her family called her as a child, lived with relatives. Her brother died at age four. Lee and her sister, Annis, went to live with her uncle, Robert Hazen, in Lula, Mississippi. Lee attended a one-room school there for most of her school years.[1]

In order to have the necessary requirements to enter college, Lee took private lessons in most of the high school subjects and read extensively on her own. In 1910, she graduated from the Mississippi Industrial Institute and College, now called the Mississippi State University for Women, with a bachelor's degree in science. To earn money for graduate school, she taught physics and biology at Central High School in Jackson, Mississippi, for six years. During her summer vacations from high school teaching, she attended classes at the University of Tennessee and the University of Virginia. Hazen applied the credits from these courses toward a master of science degree in bacteriology, which she received from Columbia University in New York City in 1917.

During World War I, she worked in the army's diagnostic laboratory as a technician. After the war, she continued her work in a laboratory in West Virginia. In 1927, Hazen became one of very few women to earn a Ph.D. degree in microbiology from Columbia University. She was forty-two years old.

She joined a team of researchers at the New York State Department of Health who were working on a variety of health problems related to bacteria-caused diseases. She helped find the source for an outbreak of anthrax. She also identified a toxin in canned seafood that had caused several deaths.[2]

There are many different kinds of organisms that can cause diseases, for example, bacteria, viruses, and fungi. Scientists had learned that antibiotics like penicillin are extremely useful in killing bacteria, however, antibiotics do not help in destroying fungi-causing diseases like ringworm and athlete's foot. In fact, one of the problems with many antibiotics is that in addition to destroying the bacteria causing an illness, they can also kill beneficial bacteria found in the body. As part of her work at the State Department of Health, Hazen began to study different kinds of fungi. Fungi are everywhere—in the air, in the water, in the ground, and even in the body. Fungi fascinated Hazen. She wanted to find a way to kill the fungi-causing diseases in humans without producing harmful side effects. She started to collect and identify a wide variety of different fungi.[3]

Rachel Fuller Brown

Rachel Fuller Brown was born in Springfield, Massachusetts, on November 23, 1898. She and her brother, Sumner, spent much of their childhood in Webster Groves, Missouri, where her father, George, worked in insurance and real estate. As a young child, Rachel loved to draw and paint. She also liked to collect insects.[4]

When Rachel was fourteen, her father left the family. Rachel's mother, Annie, decided to move her family back to Springfield, Massachusetts, to be closer to her own sisters and brothers. Soon after their return to Springfield, Rachel's grandparents came to live with the family. Because Rachel's mother now had two more people to support, the family was very poor.

Rachel's aunts and uncles convinced Annie Brown to send Rachel to the commercial high school in Springfield. They hoped that Rachel would learn skills needed to get a job after graduation and help support the family. Rachel tried the commercial studies for one semester, but she did not like her classes. Rachel transferred to the regular high school, where she took courses to prepare her for college instead. She was happier in her new school.[5] Throughout high school, her favorite subject was history.

During her senior year, she decided that she wanted to go to Mount Holyoke College in nearby

South Hadley, Massachusetts. Rachel's family was too poor to send Rachel to college. Fortunately, a friend of Rachel's grandmother, Henrietta Dexter, offered to pay Rachel's full tuition at Mount Holyoke.

When Rachel started classes, she intended to major in history. As one of the courses required for graduation, Rachel had to take a science course. She chose chemistry. This class excited her so much that she decided to have two majors: history and chemistry. She graduated from Mount Holyoke in 1920.

With continued support from her grandmother's friend, Rachel Brown went to the University of Chicago, where she received her master of science degree in organic chemistry.

Rachel did not want to rely on the goodwill of Henrietta Dexter for more money to continue her education, so she taught chemistry and physics at the Francis Shimer School, a junior college outside of Chicago. She discovered that she did not like teaching. As soon as she was able to afford to continue her education, she left teaching and entered the Ph.D. program in organic chemistry at the University of Chicago.

After Brown had finished the course work for the degree and had completed all the written work on her dissertation, the only requirement left was the oral part of her dissertation. For unknown reasons, this oral presentation was delayed.[6] Unfortunately, Brown could not wait for the decision about when the oral presentation was to be scheduled. She was running out of money and needed to find a job soon. So without completing her Ph.D., she went to work for the New York State Health Department in Albany, New York.

Seven years later, after Brown had become famous, the University of Chicago allowed her to give her oral presentation. However, her oral presentation was about her current research, not her original research. Finally, when Brown was thirty-five years old, the University of Chicago granted her a Ph.D. in organic chemistry and bacteriology.

While Brown worked at the Health Department, she was involved in various research projects. Some of the research involved searching for a simple way to test for syphilis, a sexually transmitted disease, and finding a cure for pneumonia. She then joined a team that was searching for microorganisms in soil that would kill harmful bacteria.

The Team

While Brown was in Albany looking for microorganisms in soil that would kill bacteria, Hazen was in New York City searching for microorganisms in soil that would kill harmful fungi. They both worked for the New York State Department of Health. In 1948, Brown and Hazen became a team. However, they remained in their own laboratories 150 miles apart. They shared the work by mail, sending samples back and forth.

Hazen made cultures of soil samples found all over the world. When she found a culture that seemed to stop the growth of a fungus, she mailed it to Brown. Then Brown would try to find out just what substance in the culture acted against the fungus. When she separated out the substance, she sent it back to Hazen to test again. When they found a substance that looked promising, Hazen tested it on mice. If the substance was toxic, or poisonous, to the mice, they continued their search.

In 1949, Brown and Hazen reported that they had discovered a substance that was effective against sixteen fungi and only mildly toxic to laboratory mice. By 1950, they had shown that they had an antifungal substance that was not toxic to rats or guinea pigs. The original name for this discovery was "fungicidin." They later changed the name to "nystatin" to honor their **N**ew **Y**ork **Stat**e laboratory. The sample of soil that contained the now famous microorganism came from a clump of earth Hazen had picked up in a field in Virginia where she was visiting friends.

The process of obtaining a patent for their discovery was very difficult. No pharmaceutical company would produce nystatin without a patent. Many people worked hard in collaboration to help Brown and Hazen file their patent. On February 1, 1951, Brown and Hazen filed for their patent on fungicidin. On February 27, E. R. Squibb and Sons, a drug company, signed a five-year contract to

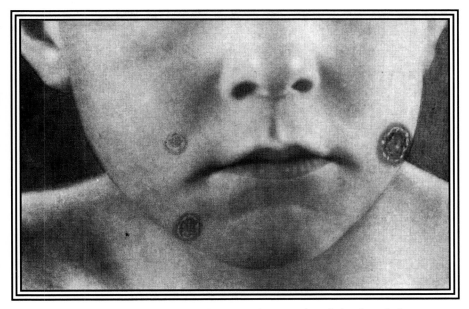

Elizabeth Hazen and Rachel Brown discovered and developed the first effective treatment for fungal diseases. One example of fungal infection, ringworm, is shown here. The areas of ringworm on the child's face are circled.

manufacture and sell the drug under the name Mycostatin. Nystatin, known as a wonder drug, became the world's first successful fungus-fighting antibiotic. Nystatin cures infections of the skin and digestive system. It also cures the Dutch Elm disease that was killing many majestic elm trees and even restores artwork damaged by water and mold.[7] During the early production of nystatin, Brown and Hazen regularly visited the New Jersey plant to make suggestions about producing the drug.

Half of the royalties from their patent, around $13 million, went to the nonprofit Research Corporation of New York, which had assisted them in obtaining a patent for their drug. These royalties helped future scientists and inventors by providing the necessary funds for research. The other half of the royalties went into the Brown-Hazen Fund, which they set up to help young college students study the biological sciences, particularly microbiology, immunology, and biochemistry.[8]

Elizabeth Hazen died on June 24, 1975, at the age of eighty-nine.[9]

Brown continued to lecture and work on her research. On January 14, 1980, Rachel Brown died. She was eighty-one.

Katherine Burr Blodgett
(1898–1979)
Research Physicist and Chemist

In 1938, the media announced that Katherine Blodgett had invented "invisible glass."[1] In fact, what she had invented was a chemical process for covering glass with a very thin film, the thickness of one or more molecules. Light was then able to go through the glass without reflecting from the surface. This caused the glass to look as if it were invisible.[2]

Katherine Burr Blodgett was born in Schenectady, New York, on January 10, 1898. She never knew her father because he had died a few weeks before she was born. In spite of his absence in her life, her father, George, who had been a patent attorney for the General Electric Company in upstate New York, influenced her.

Katherine Burr Blodgett

Katie, as she was affectionately called by her family and friends, had the opportunity to attend several fine private schools.[3] Katie's mother moved the family to New York City for three years and then to France for four years. Katie's mother wanted her children to experience and learn about the French culture. The family returned to the United States when Katie was eight years old, and Katie went to school in Saranac Lake, New York. One of her favorite subjects was math.

Throughout her young life, Katie's family frequently traveled back and forth to Europe. Finally, as a teenager, Katie went to the Rayson School for well-bred young ladies in New York City. With a scholarship to Bryn Mawr College near Philadelphia, Pennsylvania, Katherine Blodgett graduated from high school at age fifteen.[4]

At Bryn Mawr she found teachers who challenged her, like mathematician Charlotte Angas Scott and physicist James Barnes. Her physics professor inspired her to think about a career in science. This was not an easy path for a young woman at the beginning of the twentieth century.

While she was in college, she visited her father's company, General Electric (GE). An old friend of her father's, chemist Irving Langmuir, showed her around GE's research laboratory. Langmuir encouraged Blodgett to continue her education in science.[5] Blodgett graduated second in her class from Bryn

Mawr in 1917 and went to graduate school at the University of Chicago to study chemistry.

At the time Blodgett was attending graduate school in Chicago, the United States was engaged in World War I. To help the war effort, Blodgett's work focused on harmful gases. Blodgett helped to develop a gas mask that used coconut oil and charcoal to filter out the poisonous gases. This research was part of her master's degree program in chemistry. She graduated from the University of Chicago at the age of twenty-one.

Until that time, women scientists had difficulty finding work in the scientific fields. World War I changed that. With so many men serving in the military, many positions in a wide variety of scientific fields became available to women. Several important people working at General Electric knew about Blodgett's contribution to the development of the gas mask. General Electric hired Blodgett as their first female research scientist. She started her career there as Langmuir's research assistant.

One of the first projects that they worked on together was the study of tungsten. Tungsten is a metal that was used in electric light bulbs. They studied how hydrogen and oxygen formed films on the tungsten. They were interested in finding out how different amounts of heat affected these films. The studies of these films at different temperatures were important in the production of long-lasting light bulbs.

After the end of World War I, Langmuir encouraged Blodgett to go to Cambridge University in England to study with the famous physicist Sir Ernest Rutherford at the Cavendish Laboratory.[6] In 1926, she received a Ph.D. in physics from Cambridge University.

After Blodgett returned to General Electric from England, Langmuir asked her to study surface chemistry. Surface chemistry is the study of the thin layer of molecules on the surface of liquids and solids. Langmuir, in his own earlier studies, had discovered that a thin film of oil floating on water is only one molecule thick. He also discovered that these thin layers acted in a very peculiar way. They seemed to behave as if they had only two dimensions rather than three. Scientists thought that all solids had three dimensions: height, length, and width. This led Langmuir to conclude that the height of this thin layer would determine the height of one molecule.

Later, Langmuir received the Nobel Prize for this discovery. Langmuir had developed the theory about the two-dimensional quality of thin layers—only one molecule thick—but his discovery had no practical applications. Blodgett began a series of experiments to see if this theory about thin layers could be used in some practical way.

By 1933, Blodgett had developed a process to build these single molecule layers, one on top of the other. She had lowered a metal plate into some ordinary tap water on which she had floated a film of special oil called oleic acid. The thin film coated the metal plate in an even single layer as the plate went down into the water. She thought that when she pulled the plate out of the water the oleic acid would float back on the top of the water. Instead, another layer formed.

During the process, she noticed that each time that she added a layer, the new layer reflected a different color of light. She was able to determine the thickness of the film based on the color of the reflection. The thickness of these films is very small, the length of one molecule up to the length of a few molecules. General Electric turned her discovery into a product—a gauge that measures thicknesses down to a millionth of an inch.

They sold these gauges to the scientific community. These new thickness gauges were much less expensive, much more accurate, and much easier to use than similar gauges that had been available up until that time.

In addition to the film experiments, Blodgett and Langmuir also built the first large analog computer at General Electric. They used this computer to study the paths taken by particles near fibers. Katherine Blodgett and Irving Langmuir continued to work together for six more years.

Layers one molecule thick fascinated Blodgett, so she continued this research. On March 16, 1938, Blodgett received the patent for her most famous invention, "Film Structure and Method of

Preparation."[7] She discovered that when she piled up forty-four monomolecular (one molecule) layers of liquid soap on a plate of glass, the glass no longer reflected light. The popular media called her invention invisible glass, but the glass really was not invisible. It just did not reflect any light. Ninety-nine percent of the light that hit the surface of the glass went through the glass without distortion and without reflecting back.

One of the first commercial applications of Blodgett's nonreflecting glass was in the lens of a movie projector used to show the film *Gone With the Wind.* Her invention also helped makers of eyeglasses, telescopes, and microscopes develop these items so that light could pass through the lens or glass with less distortion. This "invisible glass" was important in the development of periscopes, range finders, and aerial cameras used during World War II.

When World War II started, Blodgett again refocused her research for the war effort. The army needed a dense smoke that would allow soldiers to hide from enemy attack. She created exactly what they needed. She developed a way to create a fog from two quarts of oil. This smoke screen saved the lives of many Allied soldiers serving in North Africa and Italy during the war.

With the number of planes flying in wintry conditions increasing, there was a need for a way to deice the wings of the planes. Again, this was very

One of the first uses of Katherine Blodgett's nonreflecting glass was in submarine periscopes in World War II. This officer is at the periscope in the control room of a submarine in 1942.

important during the war. Blodgett helped develop a method for deicing airplane wings.[8]

Throughout her life, Katherine Blodgett earned many honorary degrees and received many awards. In 1951, Blodgett became the first industrial scientist to win the Garvan Medal of the American Chemical Society. Also, in that same year, the mayor of Schenectady, New York, declared June 13 as Katherine Blodgett Day. In the announcement of the event, she was described as "a tireless and disciplined worker . . . a cheerful and witty colleague . . . a leading citizen with a social conscience and a deep sense of civic responsibility."[9]

Blodgett was not all seriousness and hard work. Although some described her as "a quiet, unassuming person, who seldom talked about herself,"[10] she loved to cook and garden. She acted in Schenectady's community theater group. She also liked to write silly verses and funny words for old songs.

She retired from General Electric in 1963 and spent as much time as possible at her home on Lake George, New York, where she continued to enjoy the beauty of the outdoors and to play bridge with her friends.

After a long and productive life as a research physicist and chemist, Katherine Blodgett died in 1979 at the age of eighty-one.

Gertrude Belle Elion

Gertrude Belle Elion
(1918–1999)
Cancer Fighter

Medical researchers have discovered drugs and treatments for many diseases that kill thousands of people each year. Unfortunately, the cure for many forms of cancer still eludes researchers. However, scientists have taken steps to cure some forms of cancer and at least reduce the number of deaths caused by this dreaded disease. One of these researchers was Gertrude Elion. She received the Nobel Prize for her work in cancer research and for the drugs that she discovered leading to the cure of some forms of cancer.

Gertrude Belle Elion was born on January 23, 1918, to Robert and Bertha Elion. Robert Elion had emigrated from Lithuania when he was twelve years old. His wife, Bertha, was also an immigrant, arriving from Russia when she was fourteen.[1] Gertrude's father studied to be a dentist and graduated from New York University School of Dentistry.

Gertrude, known as Trudy by her friends and family, enjoyed going to the opera with her father. He taught her how to love music. Her mother encouraged her to have her own career and her own bank account. Bertha Elion wanted her daughter to be financially independent.[2]

When Trudy was three, her grandfather came from Russia to live with the family. She loved her grandfather, who told her stories, took her to the park, and taught her how to speak Yiddish—the language of Jews from central and eastern Europe. Three years later, the family grew again, when Trudy's brother, Herbert, was born. To accommodate the increasing family size, the family found a larger home in the Bronx in New York.

Trudy attended public schools and thoroughly enjoyed learning about every subject. Reflecting on her life, she said, "I was a child with an insatiable thirst for knowledge and remember enjoying all of my courses almost equally."[3] She had an uncontrollable curiosity about everything and her friends called her a bookworm.

Her beloved grandfather died of cancer when Trudy was fifteen. She watched him die a slow, painful death. She decided that she was going to try to do something so that others would not have to suffer the way her grandfather had suffered.[4] Later when she went to college, she held on to her resolve to study science and research ways to treat cancer.

When Trudy was eleven, the United States suffered a great economic disaster, known as the Depression. The stock market crashed in 1929 and many people lost all of their savings. Refusing to believe the advice of his friends, Trudy's father did not sell his stocks before the crash. The Elion family was bankrupt. Fortunately, for the Elion children, this financial setback did not prevent them from eventually attending college.

Trudy graduated from high school at age fifteen in the middle of the Depression. Because the City College of New York (CCNY) offered free tuition, Trudy, and later Herbert, attended college there. Trudy majored in chemistry at Hunter College—then the women's section of the college.

While she was in college, Trudy Elion met a young man and fell in love. The young couple intended to marry, but tragedy struck. The young man became very ill with an infection of the heart valves and lining, and he died. Elion was devastated. Whether no one ever matched up to her first love, or she was too busy with her research, she never married.[5]

For many years following the stock market crash, people had difficulty finding work. In 1937, in the midst of the Depression, Elion graduated from Hunter College summa cum laude—highest honors—in chemistry. Unfortunately, the degree in chemistry did not help her in finding work.

Two forces combined to prevent Elion from finding a job—the Depression and the attitude held by some companies that women were unfit to work in scientific positions. Referring to her high honors she said, "It didn't make a particle of difference . . . There weren't many jobs, and what jobs there were, were not for women."[6]

One job interviewer told her that she could not have the job because she might distract the male workers. She tried to apply to graduate school. Again, discrimination against women in the sciences worked against her. Elion wanted to be a research scientist. She was rejected by fifteen graduate schools and turned down by industry. Not willing to be unemployed, she finally applied to secretarial school.

After her secretarial training, Elion spent seven years working at several part-time jobs. She saved every penny she could. Finally, she had enough money to apply to graduate school at New York University. She continued to work part-time, go to school in the afternoons and evenings, and do research on weekends.

Soon the United States was engaged in World War II. As the war progressed, more and more men were called into service, and jobs started to open up for women, even in the scientific fields. In 1942, Elion finally found a job in a chemistry laboratory. It was not cancer research, but at least it was in her field of chemistry. She tested food products for the A&P food store chain. However the work soon ceased to hold any interest for her, because it was not what she really wanted to do. By 1944, the war had taken its toll on male scientists. Elion found a position in chemistry research at the Burroughs Wellcome Company, working with George Hitchings for fifty dollars a week. Elion planned to stay with this new position just as long as she was learning new ideas. She never left.

While working at Burroughs Wellcome, she continued studying for her doctorate at Brooklyn Polytechnic Institute in the evenings. After two years, the dean of the school told her that she would have to attend school full-time or not at all. She did not want to give up her job, because it was so challenging and interesting and exactly what she had wanted to do. She abandoned her dream of getting a doctorate and continued to do research work at Burroughs Wellcome.

With the encouragement of Hitchings, Elion broadened her interests to include biochemistry—the study of chemical processes occurring in living organisms; pharmacology—the study of drugs and their uses; immunology—the study of the immune system; and virology—the study of viruses and viral infections. She was never bored again.

The team of Elion and Hitchings pioneered research on many new drugs. She was thirty-two when the team earned its first patent. Elion said,

"One usually doesn't think of drugs as an invention, but they are."[7] More than forty patents for drugs followed. One patent was for a drug that made it possible for people to have kidney transplants. The body's immune system rejects transplanted organs as foreign bodies. The drug azathioprine, or Imuran, which Elion helped discover, tricks the body into accepting the transplanted kidney.

Elion and Hitchings also developed a target-specific drug that made it possible to kill cancer cells without destroying normal cells. *The Boston Globe* reported that they "developed six different drugs against nine serious medical conditions and paved the way for others, including AZT, the only drug known to slow the progress of AIDS."[8]

Some of the other drugs that Elion helped develop include acyclovir (Zovirax®), the first drug used against viral herpes; Daraprim®, used to combat malaria; Zyloprim®, used to treat gout; and Septra®, used for bacterial infections.

Elion served as assistant to the director of the Division of Chemotherapy at Burroughs Wellcome from 1963 to 1967. Then she was head of experimental therapy from 1967 to 1983. Chemotherapy is the treatment for cancer that uses chemicals and drugs to destroy cancer cells without destroying other tissues and cells. Elion realized her dream and became known throughout the scientific community as a leader in the research effort to develop anticancer agents, including drugs for leukemia.

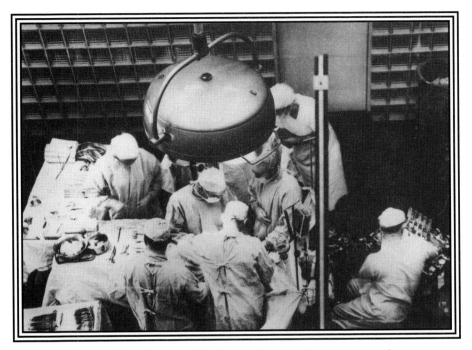

Elion's work made it possible for people to receive organ transplants without their body rejecting the new organs. Shown here is the first successful kidney transplant from a living donor in 1990.

Even though Elion never earned a Ph.D., the academic community presented her with twenty-five honorary degrees, including degrees from George Washington University, Brown University, and the University of Michigan. In 1968, the American Chemical Society awarded her the Garvan Medal for work developing drugs created to fight cancer.

The greatest award came after her 1983 retirement. In 1988, she shared the Nobel Prize in medicine with Hitchings and the British scientist Sir James Black. The Nobel Committee recognized their work in developing a series of drugs useful for treating malaria, leukemia, the immune response, viral infections, gout, and other diseases.[9] Elion received a matching prize from Burroughs Wellcome for charity. She donated the money to Hunter College for women's science education.[10]

The National Council of Intellectual Property Law Association and the United States Patent and Trademark Office established the National Inventors Hall of Fame in 1973. It was almost twenty years before they inducted woman inventors into the Hall of Fame. Gertrude Elion was the first woman inventor inducted. In 1991, upon receiving the honor she said, "I'm happy to be the first woman, but I doubt I'll be the last."[11]

Elion belonged to many work-related organizations such as the American Association for Cancer Research, the American Society of Hematology, and the American Chemical Society. She also was a fellow of the New York Academy of Sciences. She enjoyed many other activities like photography, traveling, and music. She loved to attend the opera as she had when she was a child.

Looking back on her life, she said, "I never let myself be discouraged if things went wrong. You can't let a few failures dissuade you from your purpose."[12]

Gertrude Elion continued to live an active and productive life until her death on February 20, 1999.

Stephanie Louise Kwolek
(1923–)
Polymer Chemist

Over two thousand police and other law enforcement officers have been saved because they were wearing bullet-resistant vests. What these officers probably do not know is that a woman chemist invented the material used to make their vests. In 1966, Stephanie Louise Kwolek led her research team in the hunt for a material stronger than Superman's clothes. Kwolek found that material and named it Kevlar.®

Stephanie Louise Kwolek was born in New Kensington, Pennsylvania, on July 31, 1923. Her father, John, worked as a mold maker in a foundry, but he really liked to be outside exploring nature. Stephanie and her brother went with their father on many hikes. They made collections of leaves, flowers,

Stephanie Louise Kwolek

and other interesting objects that they found along the way. Stephanie carefully sorted all these treasures of nature and kept them in scrapbooks.

From her mother, Nellie Kwolek, Stephanie learned how to do a wide variety of needlecrafts like sewing and knitting. Throughout her childhood, Stephanie enjoyed working with fabrics and designing clothes. Kwolek said, "I thought that I might be a fashion designer. I spent an awful lot of time drawing various types of clothes and sewing."[1]

From her parents, Stephanie received two of her life's greatest gifts—her fascination with science and her love of fabrics and materials. When it came time for Stephanie to decide about what she was going to do with her life, she had difficulty choosing between the two. Should she be a scientist or should she be a fashion designer?

Stephanie experienced a great loss when she was ten years old. Her father died. Nellie Kwolek had to go to work to support herself and her two children. She found a job at the Aluminum Company of America. Stephanie's mother was lucky to find work. Many people were unemployed during the 1930s because of the Depression. In spite of these very difficult times, Nellie Kwolek wanted each of her children to have a college education.

After graduating from high school in 1942, Stephanie Kwolek entered the women's college that was then part of Carnegie-Mellon University near Pittsburgh, Pennsylvania. As with many other colleges and universities in earlier years, women had not been allowed to major in certain sciences or engineering.

During World War II, many male students left college to serve in the armed forces. The war caused many college classrooms to be nearly empty. In order to fill their classrooms, Carnegie-Mellon allowed women students to take science and engineering classes. Kwolek was one of the women taking these courses. She graduated from college in 1946 with two majors: one in chemistry and one in biology.

Kwolek had studied both chemistry and biology because she was considering going to medical school and becoming a doctor. However, the cost of medical school was more than Kwolek and her family could afford.[2] She decided to find temporary employment to save enough money to continue her education.

In the years immediately following World War II, there were great shifts in the job market in the United States. Businesses and industries that had welcomed women workers during the war now tried to convince them to leave those jobs. Many employers wanted these jobs to be available for the returning servicemen. Kwolek, however, was very fortunate. She found work as a chemist for E. I. DuPont de Nemours and Company, known as DuPont. She said, "The first year, the work . . . was so challenging. I loved to solve problems, and it was a constant learning process. Each day there was something new, a new challenge, and I loved that."[3] She liked her research so much that she never thought about going back to medical school. Later she said, "I joined DuPont as a temporary measure, but the work turned out to be so interesting that I stayed on."[4]

The two interests of Kwolek's childhood, fabrics and science, came together in her work at DuPont. Kwolek worked as a research chemist in the textile fibers laboratory in Buffalo, New York, from 1946 to 1950. When the textile laboratory moved to Wilmington, Delaware, in 1950, Kwolek moved also.

Throughout the late 1940s, many women lost or gave up their wartime jobs. Although Kwolek did not lose her job, she did not receive raises or promotions. DuPont promoted younger men with less experience ahead of her. It took fifteen years before she received a promotion. She said, "My upward progress was definitely limited—there just weren't any women supervisors in research."[5] While this was disappointing, she loved her work and continued to make many new discoveries in her field. Eventually she did receive promotions, but her rate of advancement was still much slower than that of male colleagues.

Kwolek's field of research was polymer chemistry. Polymers are strings of small molecules connected together in very long chains. Protein and rubber molecules are examples of polymers that occur in nature.

Before World War II, the only sources available to make cloth were natural ones, such as wool from sheep, cotton and flax from plants, and silk from

Dr. Stephanie Kwolek prepares a new polymer in the Pioneering Research laboratory at the DuPont Company.

silkworms. In 1939, chemists had created a new polymer called nylon. When woven into cloth, it had very special properties. Unlike cotton cloth, it did not rot or absorb water, it did not need to be ironed, and it resisted abrasion, mildew, and insects. Nylon became very popular. The U.S. War Department also liked nylon because manufacturers could make parachutes more quickly and in larger quantities from nylon than from silk spun by silkworms.

Once chemists started to make fibers and materials chemically, a new field of science was born. Chemists everywhere searched for new polymers.

The chemists at DuPont produced many polymers used to make new kinds of fabrics and materials. Dacron™ polyester, Orlon™ acrylic, and Lycra® spandex were some of the fabrics invented and produced by chemists at DuPont. Kwolek was happy as she found this work exciting. She was doing chemistry, and she was helping search for fibers that could be made into new kinds of cloth.

Most chemical researchers tried to spin the new polymers into long threads at high temperatures. Kwolek chose a different path. She looked for polymers that she could spin at room temperature or low temperatures. Through her research, she became the country's leading scientist in the area of low temperature polymerization. Her team discovered and created Kapton® polymimide film and Nomex® aramid fiber. Manufacturers use Nomex to make clothing for firefighters because it is a fire-resistant fabric that provides much better protection than other materials.[6]

In 1964, DuPont wanted its chemists to find a material that would be indestructible, like Superman's clothes. Kwolek and her team experimented with solutions of polymers called liquid crystals. Liquid crystals are quite different from other polymers. In most polymers, the long chain molecules are tangled in a disorganized arrangement. In liquid crystals, however, the molecules all line up pointing in the same direction and parallel to one another.

Kwolek and her research team looked and looked for this superstrong polymer fiber. They did many experiments. One day, Kwolek made a polymer solution that did not act like any of the others. Up until then, the polymer solutions that she had been using were transparent, like glass. The new solution looked more like milk. When Kwolek and her team of research assistants tested the new fibers, they could not believe how strong it was. Kwolek thought that the tests were inaccurate. She ran the tests again. The results were the same. She had discovered a polymer that was stronger than steel.

DuPont had challenged its chemists to find a superstrong polymer. In 1966, Kwolek successfully invented the chemical process leading to the development of Kevlar®. Finally, when DuPont was ready to put her discovery on the market in 1971, she applied for the patent.

Her discovery led to a multimillion-dollar industry. Kevlar is five times stronger than steel, lighter than asbestos, and does not rust. Many different manufacturers use Kevlar in making their products, such as underwater cables, brake linings, belted tires, space vehicles, boats, and even the sails on boats. Kevlar is found in rope, thermal insulating clothing, and its most famous use, bullet-resistant vests.

Kwolek said, "Unquestionably, polymers have improved the lives of many people. It's very difficult to turn around without bumping into at least three items that contain them."[7]

After she invented Kevlar, Stephanie Kwolek went on to patent more than twenty-seven other products and processes. She patented her solvents and a new way to spin polymers. She won the American Chemical Society Award for Creative Invention in 1980 for her method of spinning fibers. Kwolek received many other awards, including the American Society of Metals Award and the Chemical Pioneer Award from the American Institute of Chemists.

She received an honorary doctor of science degree from Worcester Polytecnic Institute in 1981. In the late nineties, she was the fourth woman inducted into the National Inventors Hall of Fame. On July 26, 1996, President Bill Clinton presented her with the National Medal of Technology. She also received the Perkins Medal and the Lemelson-MIT Lifetime Achievement Award.

Since her retirement from DuPont, Kwolek remains active by offering her services as a consultant. She also travels around the country giving lectures in schools and sharing her enthusiasm for the study of science. She continues to encourage students to consider the many exciting careers available in the fields of science.

It is hard to imagine what life would be like today without the many inventions of chemist Stephanie Kwolek.

Edith Flanigen

Edith Flanigen
(1929–)
Research Chemist

Most people who are not chemists do not know what a molecular sieve is and why it is important. Molecular sieves are important because they help produce the cooling fluid in your refrigerator and the gasoline used in your cars. Chemist Edith Flanigen designed the molecular sieve called Zeolite Y, which is widely used to refine petroleum.[1]

Edith Flanigen was born in Buffalo, New York, on January 28, 1929. Her father worked in the lumber business and her mother was a homemaker. Even though neither of her parents had the opportunity to attend college, they both supported the education of their four children.

Edith attended a private Catholic high school, Holy Angels Academy in Buffalo. One of her favorite classes was chemistry, taught by Sister St. Mary. The class was different from any other classes Edith had taken. In this chemistry class, Sister St. Mary allowed the students to do chemistry experiments rather than just reading about them. Actually doing science excited Edith. She loved learning about what happens when you put chemicals together. Her experience in this class helped her to decide about her future. She chose chemistry as her life's work.

Sister St. Mary also influenced Edith's sisters. They too found chemistry exciting. Three of the four Flanigen children, Jane, Edith, and Joan, grew up to have careers in chemistry. The three Flanigen sisters majored in chemistry at D'Youville College in Buffalo, New York.

In addition to her studies in chemistry, Edith had many other interests. While at D'Youville, she belonged to the National Federation of Catholic College students. She served as president of her college class. Even with these outside activities, she still managed to graduate from college in 1950 as valedictorian, the student with the highest grades in the graduating class. Along with her sister Joan, Edith Flanigen continued her education at Syracuse University, where they both worked on master's degrees in chemistry.

While at Syracuse, Edith had a terrible accident. Someone had left the valve on a tank of acetylene gas open. Because of the design of the handle, it looked as if it were at zero pressure rather than at full pressure. When Edith lit the torch on the tank, it blew up. She badly burned her hands. She spent the rest of the semester in the infirmary as her burns slowly healed. Her sister Joan went to all of Edith's classes to take notes for her, so that Edith would not miss any of her class work.[2]

The accident could have been worse. Fortunately, Edith's lab coat protected the rest of her body from serious burns. The experience led her to think seriously about hazards in chemistry laboratories. She says that the accident caused her to be "extremely religious about laboratory safety."[3]

Following graduation from Syracuse, Edith Flanigen worked as a research chemist for the Union Carbide Corporation in Tonawanda, New York. There were not many women working as research chemists in the 1950s. However, at one time, all three Flanigen sisters were working for Union Carbide as chemists. It was amazing that three women from the same family were working for the same company as research chemists.

When Edith Flanigen joined Union Carbide in the Linde Division in 1952, she first worked on the chemistry of the element silicone. By 1956, Flanigen had moved to join a team working on molecular sieves.

In the 1960s, the government was funding maser research. Masers (**M**icrowave **A**mplification by **S**timulated **E**mission of **R**adiation) are devices that amplify or generate electromagnetic waves. The United States was hoping that emeralds might be used as a new maser crystal material. This research required very large, high quality emerald crystals. The Linde Company already had developed the technique for growing synthetic sapphires. The government awarded a contract to the Linde Company to find a way to grow perfect emeralds.

Flanigen and her coworker, Norbert Mumbach, developed a process for making emeralds. They dissolved different compounds of aluminum, silicon, beryllium, and chromium in water. The temperature and the pressure of the solutions were very carefully controlled. With patience and accurate control, they were able to grow perfect emeralds very slowly at a rate of one micron per day. A micron is one-thousandth of a millimeter. A millimeter is the smallest unit on most metersticks. The Linde Company sold some of these perfect emeralds that had grown for five to ten years for jewelry.

Flanigen's most important contributions, however, had begun in the late 1950s when she joined the team working in a new research area called molecular sieves. These sieves are solid crystalline structures. They have very small holes of equal size that will just allow molecules smaller than the pores to pass through the solid. This technology provides a way to separate small molecules from mixtures containing larger molecules.

Flanigen's early work in making these crystalline materials produced a special set of compounds composed of aluminum, phosphorus, and oxygen,

The petroleum refining industry uses Flanigen's sieve to separate crude oil into parts, such as gasoline and heating oil.

commonly referred to as zeolite Y. The petroleum refining industry made extensive use of zeolite Y in the process of separating crude oil as it comes from the ground into different parts, such as gasoline and heating oil. Scientists use different forms of zeolite Y for selecting the desired sizes of molecules from mixtures.[4]

Some forms of zeolite also have a different application as a catalyst. A catalyst is a substance that is able to speed up a chemical reaction. Flanigen found that a form of zeolite would speed up the "cracking" process used with crude oil. The cracking process enables oil refineries to take large molecules that are not needed and break them apart to form more desirable molecules for gasoline and jet fuel.[5] The contribution of Flanigen to the petroleum industry has helped to produce fuels that are more economical and better for the environment.

Work on sieves is important in many areas besides petroleum refinement. They are also useful in water purification and for cleaning up environmental contamination. Flanigen and her colleagues had developed a whole new generation of molecular sieve materials. She holds 104 U.S. patents for her work, which led to a completely new set of materials used in making molecular sieves.

Union Carbide named Flanigen as its first woman Senior Corporate Research Fellow in 1982. Ten years later, Flanigen earned the Perkins Medal for work on sieves. She was the first woman to receive the medal in its eighty-six year history.

After forty-two years of outstanding research, more than one hundred patents, and the development of over two hundred different synthetic compounds, Flanigen retired from Union Carbide in 1994. That same year, she received the Inaugural International Zeolite Association Award for Outstanding Lifetime Contributions to and Achievements in the Field of Zeolites.[6] Since her retirement, Flanigen continues to be active in many professional organizations. She travels extensively around the world delivering lectures about zeolite.

Ellen Ochoa
(1958–)
Astronaut

At NASA Mission Control in Houston, the music of Mozart and Vivaldi filled the room. The music was coming from the Discovery Space Shuttle Mission STS-56. Astronaut Ellen Ochoa was playing her flute as she watched Earth pass beneath her.

Ellen Ochoa was born in Los Angeles on May 10, 1958, to Rosanne Deardorff and Joseph Ochoa. She spent most of her childhood in La Mesa, California, which she considers her hometown. Her parents divorced while Ellen was in junior high school, leaving her mother with five children: two girls and three boys.

Throughout her childhood, Ellen loved music, math, and science. She also excelled in all her other subjects. When she was thirteen, she won the San

Astronaut and inventor Ellen Ochoa with her then one-year-old son, Wilson, after returning from her spaceflight.

Diego County spelling bee. In both seventh and eighth grades, her junior high school named her as their most outstanding student. She attended Grassmont High School in La Mesa. While in high school, she pursued many interests, particularly music. Grassmont High School selected her as their top musician. When she graduated from high school as valedictorian (the top of her class) in 1975, she continued her studies at nearby San Diego State University.

Ochoa enjoyed doing so many things that she had a difficult time deciding what career to choose. After trying out five different college majors, she chose physics.[1] She wanted to use her math skills to understand and explain the physical world. While she was in college, she played in the school's marching band and the woodwind ensemble. She qualified for Phi Beta Kappa and Sigma Xi, both honor societies for students who had excellent grades. Ochoa graduated from San Diego State University as valedictorian in 1980, with a bachelor of science degree. She loved music and science equally and could not decide whether to become a professional musician or to find a career in science. Her mother convinced her to continue her college education before choosing a career.

Ellen started her graduate studies in electrical engineering at Stanford University, where she focused on optics, the study of light. Ochoa began designing optical systems that could look at an object, analyze it, and then draw conclusions about it. These optical detection systems are able to find small objects in larger images.[2] Eventually as coinventor, she received three patents for optical inspection systems. One system inspects objects, one identifies and can "recognize" them, and one makes the images of the objects clearer.[3] These patents are for "novel ways of finding visual needles in haystacks no matter where the needles are or which way they are pointing."[4] These techniques help scientists by making clearer pictures from the information sent back from space.

In 1983, while Ochoa was in graduate school at Stanford University, Sally Ride became the first American woman astronaut. At that point, Ochoa decided she wanted to become an astronaut also. When she graduated from Stanford University in 1985 with a Ph.D. in electrical engineering, Ochoa continued her work on optical scanning at Sandia National Laboratory in Albuquerque, New Mexico. At Sandia and the National Aeronautics and Space Administration Ames Research Center in Mountain View, California, Ochoa pursued her interest in computer programs that model events in space. These programs were an extension of the optical scanning designs that she had started in graduate school. While at Ames, she served as chief of the Intelligent Systems Technology Branch, supervising thirty-five engineers and scientists. This work included designing computer systems for trips into space.

Ochoa had experience in designing computer hardware as well as expertise in optics. These skills were important to NASA. Pursuing her dream of becoming an astronaut, Ochoa applied to NASA's astronaut training program. In 1990, in addition to marrying Coe Fulmer Miles of Molalla, Oregon, Ellen Ochoa became the first Hispanic woman astronaut.

Ochoa served as mission specialist on Discovery Space Shuttle Mission STS-56, a nine-day mission, in April 1993. While traveling in space, Ochoa played her flute. She said, "You can hold the music up and you don't even need a music stand."[5] She played Vivaldi and Mozart on her flute as she watched Earth pass beneath her. "It's a very fond memory," says Ellen. "It was just very peaceful." She also played "The Marine Corps Hymn" for Ken Cameron, the Marine Corps colonel commanding the mission.[6]

A year later, Ochoa was payload commander on Shuttle Mission STS-66, an eight-day space flight. On these missions, Ochoa studied the effect of the sun on Earth's atmosphere and climate. Recording the energy of the sun during part of its eleven-year solar cycle is important in learning how changes in the sun's energy affect Earth's climate and environment. This information is necessary for scientists who are studying the damage that has been done to Earth's ozone layer. The ozone layer in the atmosphere lies about twenty to thirty miles above Earth's surface.

It protects plants and animals from the harmful ultraviolet rays of the sun.

In 1998, Ochoa gave birth to a son, Wilson. On Wilson's first birthday, Ochoa was preparing for Mission STS-96. It is very difficult being a mother and an astronaut. She says, "I just spent as much time with him as I could when we were not training."[7] Ochoa's mission required her to spend three weeks away from her one-year old son. She did not want Wilson to forget her, so she made a videotape of herself that her husband played for Wilson every night that she was away.

On Mission STS-96, a ten-day mission, she and the crew made the first docking to the International Space Station (ISS). They also delivered four tons of supplies. These supplies were for the crew who would live on the space station. Ochoa coordinated transfer of supplies, and the crew accomplished their mission in 153 orbits of Earth. The crew traveled 4 million miles in 235 hours and 13 minutes.

During this mission, Ochoa operated the RMS, a fifty-foot robot arm, during an eight-hour space walk. She used the RMS to remove a satellite from the cargo bay and place it in orbit. A day later, Ochoa used the arm to catch the satellite and bring it back into the shuttle.

While the satellite was circling Earth, it collected data about the sun and about the solar wind. The solar wind is a stream of electrons and protons that comes from the sun and enter Earth's atmosphere, mostly

Crew members of the STS-96 after completion of an assignment at the International Space Station. Ochoa is on the bottom, right.

around the North and South poles. When many electrons and protons reach either the North or South Pole at the same time, the night sky around the Pole glows with brilliant colors of light. Around the North Pole, this effect is known as the aurora borealis, or northern lights. In the Southern Hemisphere, it is called the aurora australis.

Ellen Ochoa has many talents and interests, all of which she thoroughly enjoys. She has her pilot's license and loves to fly private planes. She also bicycles and plays volleyball. In spite of her very busy life as wife, mother, astronaut, and computer systems engineer, she still has time to belong to the Optical Society of America and the American Institute of Aeronautics and Astronautics.

By the first year of the new millennium, at forty-three, Ochoa already had coinvented three systems valuable to space travel, traveled in space three times, and had won a number of awards: From NASA, she received the Exceptional Service Medal (1997), the Outstanding Leadership Medal (1995), Space Flight Medals (1999, 1994, 1993), and two Space Act Tech Brief Awards (1992). She also received the Women in Aerospace Outstanding Achievement Award, the Hispanic Engineer Albert Baez Award for Outstanding Technical Contribution to Humanity, and the Hispanic Heritage Leadership Award.[8]

San Diego State University awarded Ochoa the Alumna of the Year award. In 1993, Ochoa took this medallion into space with her. She wanted to honor her alma mater because she was so thankful for the education she had received as a student there.

Ellen Ochoa believes that hard work, motivation, and persistence, as well as support from her parents, helped her succeed in work and school.[9]

Chapter Notes

Introduction

1. Deborah Merritt, "Hypatia in the Patent Office: Women Inventors and the Law, 1865–1900," *The American Journal of Legal History,* vol. XXXV (Philadelphia: Temple University School of Law, 1991), p. 237.

2. Susan Casey, *Women Invent: Two Centuries of Discoveries That Have Shaped Our World* (Chicago: Chicago Review Press, Inc., 1997), p. 8.

3. J. E. Bedi, "Exploring the History of Women Inventors," *Lemelson Center Invention Features: Women Inventors,* n.d., <http://www.si.edu/lemelson/centerpieces/ililves/women inventors.html> (July 11, 2003).

Chapter 1. The First American Women Inventors

1. John H. Lienhard, "No. 384: Samuel Slater,"<http://www.uh.edu/engines/epi384.htm> (February 21, 2001).

2. The Library of Congress, "Mary Kies Became the First Woman to Receive a U.S. Patent, May 5, 1809," n.d., <http://www.americaslibrary.gov/cgi-bin/page.cgi/jb/nation/maryk_1> (July 11, 2003).

3. Susan Casey, *Women Invent: Two Centuries of Discoveries That Have Shaped Our World* (Chicago: Chicago Review Press, Inc., 1997), p. 66.

4. What You Need to Know About, "Margaret Knight—Queen of Paper Bags (Mary Bellis)" ©2003. <http://inventors.about.com/library/inventors/blknight.htm> (July 11, 2003).

5. Marilyn Ogilvie and Joy Harvey, eds., *The Biographical Dictionary of Women in Science: Pioneering Lives from Ancient Times to the Mid-20th Century,* vol. 1 (New York: Routledge, 2000), p. 707.

6. Arlene Hambrick, *Biographies of Black Female Scientists and Inventors: An Interdisciplinary Middle School Curriculum Guide: "What Shall I Tell My Children Who Are Black?"* Unpublished doctoral dissertation (Amherst, Mass.: University of Massachusetts, 1993), p. 91.

7. Hambrick, p. 102–112.

8. Anne MacDonald, *Feminine Ingenuity* (New York: Ballantine Books, 1992), p. 249.

Chapter 2. Madam C. J. Walker

1. Linda J. Altman, *Women Inventors* (New York: Facts On File, Inc., 1997), p. 38.

2. A'Lelia Bundles, *On Her Own Ground* (New York: Scribner, 2001), p. 64.

3. Ibid., p. 60.

4. Ethlie Ann Vare and Greg Ptacek, *Women Inventors & Their Discoveries* (Minneapolis: The Oliver Press, 1993), p. 58.

5. The Faces of Science: African Americans in the Sciences, "Madame C. J. Walker: Inventor, Businesswoman" © 1995–2000, <http://www.princeton.edu/~mcbrown/display/walker. html> (February 19, 2001).

6. Women's History Month: Spotlight on Women's History, "Madam C. J. Walker (Sarah Breedlove)," n.d., <http://www.senate.gov/~landrieu/whm/walker.html> (July 11, 2003).

7. What You Need to Know About, "Madame C. J. Walker (1867–1919) (Mary Bellis)" © 2003, <http://www.inventors.about.com/science/inventors/library/inventors/bl walker.htm> (February 19, 2001).

8. Vare and Ptacek, p. 65.

Chapter 3. Lillian Gilbreth

1. Lillian Gilbreth, *As I Remember* (Norcross, Geor.: Engineering and Management Press, 1998), p. 24.

2. Doug Benner, "Engineering Hero: Dr. Lillian M. Gilbreth," http://www.njspe.org/75a_Gilbreth.htm (March 31, 2001).

3. Inventor of the Week, "Women Invent for Women," March 1997, <http://web.mit.edu/invent/iow/whm3.html> (March 31, 2001).

4. Edna Yost, *Frank and Lillian Gilbreth: Partners for Life* (New Brunswick, N.J.: Rutgers University Press, 1949), p. 333.

Chapter 4. Beulah Henry

1. Susan Casey, *Women Invent: Two Centuries of Discoveries That Have Shaped Our World* (Chicago: Chicago Review Press, Inc., 1997), p. 46.

2. What You Need to Know About, "Beulah Henry," © 2003, <http://inventors.about.com/library/inventors/bl beulah.htm> (July 11, 2003).

3. J. E. Bedi, "Exploring the History of Women Inventors," *Lemelson Center Invention Features: Women Inventors*, n.d. <http://www.si.edu/lemelson/centerpieces/ililves/women inventors.html> (November 7, 2000).

4. Ibid.

5. Casey, p. 46.

6. Innovative Lives, "Exploring the History of Women Inventors (JE Bedi)" March 14, 2002, <http://www.si.edu/ lemelson/centerpieces/ilives/womeninventors.html> (November 7, 2000).

7. Ibid.

8. Anne MacDonald, *Feminine Ingenuity* (New York: Ballantine Books, 1992), p. 296.

9. Ibid., p. 297.

10. Ibid., p. 296.

11. Casey, p. 47.

Chapter 5. Elizabeth Lee Hazen and Rachel Fuller Brown

1. Marilyn Ogilvie and Joy Harvey, eds., *The Biographical Dictionary of Women in Science: Pioneering Lives from Ancient Times to the Mid-20th Century*, vol. 1 (New York: Routledge, 2000), p. 573.

2. Elizabeth O'Hern, *Profiles of Pioneer Women Scientists* (Washington, D.C.: Acropolis Books Ltd., 1985), p. 96.

3. Richard S. Baldwin, *The Fungus Fighters* (Ithaca, N.Y.: Cornell University Press, 1981), p. 45.

4. Ibid., p. 46.

5. Ibid., p. 47ff.

6. Autumn Stanley, *Mothers and Daughters of Invention: Notes for a Revised History of Technology* (New Brunswick, N.J.: Rutgers University Press, 1995), p. 128.

7. Hall of Fame/Inventor Profile, "Elizabeth Lee Hazen," © 2002, <http://www.invent.org/hall_of_fame/75.html> (January 2, 2001).

8. Anne MacDonald, *Feminine Ingenuity* (New York: Ballantine Books, 1992), p. 354.

9. Baldwin, p. 186.

Chapter 6. Katherine Burr Blodgett

1. Anne MacDonald, *Feminine Ingenuity* (New York: Ballantine Books, 1992), p. 310.

2. Patricia J. Siegel and K. Thomas Finley, *Women in the Scientific Search: An American Bio-Bibliography,* 1724–1979 (Metuchen, N.J.: Scarecrow Press, 1985), p. 69.

3. Linda J. Altman, *Women Inventors.* (New York: Facts On File, 1997), p. 64.

4. Ibid., p. 65.

5. Benjamin F. Shearer and Barbara S. Shearer, eds., *Notable Women in the Physical Sciences: A Biographical Dictionary* (Westport, Conn.: Greenwood Press, 1997), p. 22.

6. Siegel and Finley, p. 66.

7. Inventor of the Week, "Stephanie Louise Kwolek," April 1999, <http://web.mit.edu/invent/iow/kwolek.html> (March 27, 2001).

8. Emily J. McMurray, ed., *Notable Twentieth-Century Scientists* (Detroit, Mich.: Gale Research, 1995), p. 199.

9. Shearer and Shearer, p. 24.

10. Marilyn Ogilvie and Joy Harvey, eds., *The Biographical Dictionary of Women in Science: Pioneering Lives from Ancient Times to the Mid-20th Century,* vol. 1 (New York: Routledge, 2000), p. 149.

Chapter 7. Gertrude Belle Elion

1. Benjamin F. Shearer and Barbara S. Shearer, eds. *Notable Women in the Physical Sciences: A Biographical Dictionary* (Westport, Conn.: Greenwood Press, 1997), p. 85.

2. Sharon B. McGrayne, *Nobel Prize Women in Science* (Secaucus, N.J.: Carol Publishing Group, 1998), p. 285.

3. Nobel e-Museum, "Gertrude B. Elion—Autobiography," 1988, <http://www.nobel.se/medicine/ laureates/1988/elion-autobio.html> (January 2, 2001).

4. Susan Casey, *Women Invent: Two Centuries of Discoveries That Have Shaped Our World* (Chicago: Chicago Review Press, Inc., 1997), p. 49.

5. Miles Goodman, *Women in Chemistry and Physics,* Louis Grinstein, Rose K. Rose, and Miriam Rafailovich, eds., (Westport, Conn., Greenwood Press, 1993), p. 175.

6. McGrayne, p. 287.

7. Casey, p. 49.

8. *The Boston Globe,* "Honoring Drug Discoveries" © 1997, <http://www.boston.com/globe/search/stories/nobel/1988/1988j.html> (January 2, 2001).

9. Goodman, p. 72.

10. Marilyn Ogilvie and Joy Harvey, eds., *The Biographical Dictionary of Women in Science: Pioneering Lives from Ancient Times to the Mid-20th Century,* vol. 1 (New York: Routledge, 2000), p. 416.

11. Casey, p. 51.

12. Casey, p. 49.

Chapter 8. Stephanie Louise Kwolek

1. Innovative Lives, "Kevlar, the Wonder Fiber (Caitlyn Howell)," April 16, 1999, <http://www.si.edu/lemelson/center pieces/ilives/lecture05.html> (January 2, 2001).

2. Ibid.

3. Ibid.

4. Hall of Fame/Inventor Profile, "Stephanie Louise Kwolek," © 2002, <http://www.invent.org/hall_of_fame/90.html> (December 12, 2000).

5. Anne MacDonald, *Feminine Ingenuity* (New York: Ballantine Books, 1992), p. 374.

6. The Great Idea Finder, "Stephanie L. Kwolek," January 29, 2003, <http://www.ideafinder.com/history/inventors/kwolek.htm> (December 12, 2000).

7. Inventor of the Week, "Stephanie Louise Kwolek," April 1999, <http://web.mit.edu/invent/iow/kwolek.html> (March 27, 2001).

Chapter 9. Edith Flanigen

1. What You Need to Know About, "Edith Flanigen (Mary Bellis)," © 2003, (March 6, 2001) <http://inventors.about.com/library/inventors/blflanigen.htm> (March 6, 2001).

2. Ibid.

3. Ibid.

4. ADCOA: Absorbents & Desiccants Corporation of America, "Molecular Sieve," ©2003, <http://www.thomas register.com/olc/adcoa/molecula.htm> (March 6, 2001).

5. Inventor of the Week, "Edith M. Flanigen," March 1997, <http://www.mit.edu/afs/athena.mit.edu/org/invent/iow/flanigen.html> (March 6, 2001).

6. UOP, "Edith Flanigen," © 2001, <http://uop.com/solutions_and_innovation/research_and_development/prominent_researchers/edith_flanigen.html> (March 6, 2001).

Chapter 10. Ellen Ochoa

1. "Astronaut's Heart Stays Close to Home (Amy Lattarulo)" n.d., <http://www.thedailyaztec.com/Archive/Fall-1999/12-02/city/city03.html> (February 19, 2001).

2. Martha Bailey, *American Women in Science: A Biographical Dictionary* (Santa Barbara, Calif.: ABC-CLIO, 1994), p. 292.

3. Inventor of the Week, "Ellen Ochoa: Optical Analysis Systems," n.d., <http://web.mit.edu/invent/iow/ochoa.html> (January 2, 2001).

4. CNN.com Downlinks with Miles O'Brien, "Getting to Know the Crew of STS-96," May 24, 1999, <http://www.cnn.com/tech/space/9905/24/downlinks/> (January 2, 2001).

5. Ibid.

6. Ibid.

7. Ibid.

8. NASA Biographical Data, "Ellen Ochoa (Ph.D.): Deputy Director, Flight Crew Operations Johnson Space Center," January 2003, <http://www.jsc.nasa.gov/Bios/html bios/ochoa.html> (January 2, 2001).

9. Innovative Lives, "Research in Orbit," February 5, 1999, <http://www.si.edu/lemelson/centerpieces/ilives/lecture 07.html> (January 2, 2001).

Further Reading

Books

Currie, Stephen. *Women Inventors*. Farmington Hills, Ill.: Gale Group, 2001.

St. John, Jetty. *Hispanic Scientists: Ellen Ochoa, Carlos A. Ramirez, Eloy Rodriquez, Lydia Villa Kamaroff, Maria Elena Zavala*. Danbury, Conn.: Children's Press, 1996.

Sullivan, Richard, and Jim Haskins. *Black Stars: African American Women Scientists and Inventors*. New York: John Wiley & Sons, 2001.

Thimmesh, Catherine. *Girls Think of Everything: Stories of Ingenious Inventions by Women*. Boston: Houghton Mifflin, 2000.

Vare, Ethlie Ann, and Greg Ptacek. *Patently Female: From AZT to TV Dinners, Stories of Women Inventors and Their Breakthrough Ideas*. New York: John Wiley & Sons, 2001.

——. *Women Inventors and Their Discoveries*. Minneapolis, Minn.: Oliver Press, 1993.

Internet Addresses

4,000 Years of Women in Science
<http://www.astr.ua.edu/4000WS/>

Kids Cafe: #1 Guide for Elementary to High School Young Inventors
<http://kids.patentcafe.com/index.asp>

Index